Name of Celebrant:

____

Location:

____

Date:

____

Quinceanera is a tradition steeped in faith.

The dreamy days of childhood are over, and the responsibilities of womanhood beckon.

Made in the USA
Las Vegas, NV
11 September 2022

55065171R00059